PHAEDRA

Lucius Annaeus Seneca

AUTHORED by Damien Chazelle
UPDATED AND REVISED by W.C. Miller

COVER DESIGN by Table XI Partners LLC
COVER PHOTO by Olivia Verma and © 2005 GradeSaver, LLC

BOOK DESIGN by Table XI Partners LLC

Published by GradeSaver LLC, www.gradesaver.com

First published in the United States of America by GradeSaver LLC. 2008

ISBN 978-1-60259-158-5

Printed in the United States of America

For other products and additional information please visit
http://www.gradesaver.com

Table of Contents

Table of Contents

Biography of Lucius Annaeus Seneca (3 B.C. (circa)-65 A.D.)

Lucius Annaeus Seneca, often referred to as Seneca the Younger, was born around 3 B.C. in Corduba (what is now the town of Cordoba), in Spain, to a privileged family. His father was a well-regarded teacher of rhetoric in Rome. As a result, Seneca received a first-rate education, studying in Rome in the school of the Sextii and developing a reputation at a young age as a skilled orator and rhetorician.

His rise to fame was swift. He became a well-known presence in the world of law, while gaining further fame as a writer of tragedies. In 39 AD, however, he fell out of favor with the Emperor Caligula, thus commencing a downward spiral in his reputation. The Emperor Claudius accused him of committing adultery with Julia Livilla, Claudius' niece, and exiled him to Corsica in 41 AD. Nonetheless, Seneca remained active, scribing three treatises, called *Consolationes*, while in exile. In 49 AD, Claudius' wife Agrippina recommended he be invited back to Rome, and a year later he married Pompeia Paulina, a well-connected figure on the Roman scene, and became praetor.

With his newly regained standing, Seneca befriended the prefect of the guard and became tutor to the young Nero. When Nero became Emperor, Seneca was unofficially appointed as chief minister. During this time, Seneca continued to write, and he is largely credited with the reasoned and measured policies of the first half of Nero's reign. As time wore on, however, Nero's stability wavered, and friends of his were gradually able to persuade the emperor that Seneca was in fact an enemy. Disgraced, Seneca retired from public life in 62 AD and wrote the *Letters to Lucilius*. This, however, was not sufficient for Seneca's enemies, and in 65 AD he was accused of conspiring to overthrow Nero. The Emperor requested that Seneca commit suicide. Seneca complied.

Seneca wrote numerous essays, many of which are still read today, and at least nine plays: *Thyestes*, *Hercules Furens*, *Hercules Oetaeus*, *Oedipus*, *Medea*, *Agamemnon*, *Troades*, *Phoenissae*, and *Phaedra*. Whether these plays were actually performed in front of audiences in Seneca's day, however, is debatable. Many scholars contend that the plays were meant not for performance but for recitation, and the plays' block-like structures and long monologues attest to this. Adapted largely from Greek sources – mostly the works of Sophocles, Euripides, and Aeschylus – Seneca's plays proved hugely influential to Renaissance playwrights, especially those of England.

His prose, for its part, is renowned for its eloquent logic and reasoned, often compassionate, discourse. *De Ira*, for example, examines the consequences of anger and ways in which rage may be controlled; *De Clementia* posits the claim that mercy is the greatest quality a monarch can exhibit. Seneca associated himself with the school of Stoicism, and his writing profoundly influenced the essayists and philosophical writers of centuries to come – Montaigne, Erasmus, Rousseau, Calvin, among others.

About Phaedra

Seneca's *Phaedra* was modeled on Euripides' *Hippolytus*, which told roughly the same story. It is not clear whether *Phaedra* was ever performed on stage in Seneca's time. It seems likely that it was meant instead purely for recitation, as would befit its emphasis on long speeches, its small cast of characters, and its relative brevity when compared to certain Greek tragedies from which it clearly draws.

Despite this seemingly anti-dramatic quality of Seneca's play, *Phaedra*, along with other Seneca tragedies, exerted a great deal of influence on the European theater that followed. For example, Seneca used the Chorus not merely as a rhetorical tool or a character of its own but as a de facto method of organization; his plays often depict five discrete events or turns of the plot, each separated from the other by a lengthy Chorus interjection. Thus, the Chorus suggests a five-act structure, later adopted by the Renaissance stage – which, of course, did away with the Chorus for the most part.

Much of the power of *Phaedra* in particular stems from the tension between the high emotionality, the violence and passion, of its storyline and the eloquent discourse through which Seneca, a famed orator, rhetorician, and Stoic philosopher, communicates the narrative. The characters are all figures of Greek mythology: Hippolytus famed for his beauty and his love of the hunt, Phaedra known as the daughter of King Minos of Crete and Pasiphae, mother of the Minotaur. Theseus, of course, is the best-known of the play's cast, celebrated as the brave young man who rid Athens of crime, invented wrestling, and slew the Minotaur. In *Phaedra*, however, his best years lie behind him; he is in Seneca's vision a battered man, having crawled out from the underworld to find his palace beset by troubles. He is rash, hotheaded, and vengeful, with a terrible fury he does not know how to check. His wife, Phaedra, is not entirely sympathetic, but she does seem a victim of her own emotions, and Seneca even goes so far as to imply that her tormented feelings and confusion may stem in part from Theseus' harshness as a husband.

Today, *Phaedra* is one of Seneca's most widely-read works. Tight and compact, following Aristotelian form but even more elliptical in its design, it is a work of high passion reined in by carefully constructed language, one of the simplest and most brutal of ancient tragedies.

Character List

Hippolytus

Son of Theseus and the Amazonian Antiope. A lover of the hunt and of the woods, he is known to despise women. He prefers the freedoms of the wilderness to the comforts (and constraints) of civilization.

Phaedra

Theseus' wife and Hippolytus' stepmother. Daughter of Pasiphae, who fell in love with a bull and gave birth to the Minotaur, she too becomes stricken with a "sinful" desire - a lust for Hippolytus.

Theseus

King of Athens, famed for his heroic exploits, trapped in the Underworld at the play's beginning, on a quest with his friend Pirithous to capture Persephone and bring her to the mortal world. Known for his harshness, he killed his former wife Antiope, mother of Hippolytus.

The Nurse

Phaedra's wet-nurse, an old woman who at first seems a vessel of wisdom in her attempts to console and advise her mistress, but then reveals a more sinister side when she hatches a plan to falsely accuse Hippolytus of trying to rape his stepmother.

Major Themes

Lust

Phaedra's lust for Hippolytus is the play's catalyst, the engine that drives the tragedy. But lust appears in other guises throughout the narrative, sometimes more subtly. The Chorus expounds on examples of lust throughout history, pointing in particular to Diana – the goddess of chastity, no less – driven to abandon her lunar perch to seek love with the shepherd Endymion. If the goddess of chastity can fall victim to Cupid's arrows, then anyone can. Phaedra's mother mated with a bull, less by choice than by a mad desire to do so which she could not control; Theseus married the Amazonian Antiope, then killed her, then married Phaedra, then abandoned her to pursue Persephone in the depths of the underworld. Lust drives these characters and their gods and goddesses, and more often than not it spells calamity.

Womankind

Phaedra might be considered an heir to the tradition of scheming, wicked women in Greek mythology, chief among them Medea, who is frequently referred to in Seneca's play. Yet, she is undeniably presented as an empathetic character, more victim than victimizer. If anything, it is her nurse who receives the brunt of the play's blame, for it is she, despite her age and perceived wisdom, who first hatches the plan to accuse Hippolytus of raping his stepmother. That said, to view *Phaedra* as a story about innocent men deceived and attacked by women, is simplistic at best. Theseus succumbs to a passion far more destructive than Phaedra's – the passion for revenge, the desire to kill. Without stopping to think, he calls on Neptune to kill his own stepson. At the play's close, Phaedra condemns him for his "harshness" – the same harshness that led him, we learn, to kill his former wife, Antiope, Hippolytus' mother. Villainy runs across the sexes.

Nature v. Civilization

The drama in *Phaedra* occurs in two distinct locations – the palace in Athens, and the woods bordering the city. Civilization and wilderness are clearly pitted against one another, and although the on-stage action is restricted to Athens, the vision of the outlying forest looms large. We learn of Hippolytus' preference for the wild over the urban, and Phaedra is often on the brink of racing into the woods after her loved one, donning Amazonian garb. Ironically, however, Hippolytus, though compared to a wild beast at times, behaves more rationally than his peers; he rejects Phaedra's lust, and then falls victim to Theseus' deluded wrath. The Athenians fall prey to their own emotions, while the Amazonian, though he does perhaps behave rashly by fleeing into the forest, is comparatively reasoned in his actions. Civilization corrupts, as Hippolytus himself argues in a speech to the wet-nurse; the "primal age" was a time of peace, and with the rise of the city has come warfare and crime. It is doubly ironic, then, that Hippolytus' bloody death should come not by way of the city, not by way of manmade weapons, but by way of frenzied horses, a monstrous bull, and the merciless forest terrain. Hippolytus' beloved nature ultimately does him in.

Language

Seneca was renowned as an orator, and *Phaedra* is filled with eloquent monologues and clever pieces of rhetoric. The characters wield language as a weapon, as when Phaedra deceives her husband, then rubs the cruel truth in his face. Language can also be used to muddle, as when Theseus calls a response from the wet-nurse "riddling words" and demands she "speak plainly."

Hunting

Phaedra begins with a man setting out to hunt, and proceeds to examine various ways in which the notion of *hunting* might manifest itself within the walls of a city. Phaedra and her nurse seek to seduce Hippolytus, luring him to satisfy Phaedra's designs; they emerge as predators, he as prey. Phaedra, however, is likewise prey – prey to Cupid, that merciless hunter who targets all living beings with his arrows. At the end of the play, Hippolytus sees his role as hunter reversed, a bull from the sea plummeting toward him and his horses, eyes locked on the target ahead. Seneca portrays the machinations that accompany love as games akin to a forest hunt, replete with traps, snares, feints, and unexpected reversals.

The Gods

Though the gods never appear in person in *Phaedra*, they are continually invoked. Phaedra blames Venus and Apollo for her and her mother's impure lusts; Neptune follows Theseus' directive and slays Hippolytus, via a monstrous sea-bull. The Chorus notes, in one of the play's most intriguing passages, that the gods target those mortals of whom they can feel jealous. The poor and "humble" rarely feel the gods' wrath; instead, it is those in power who fall prey to the heavens. The passage is a sort of meta-moment, reflecting on the very stuff of tragedy – that is, the fall of great men and women.

Beauty

Hippolytus' beauty drives Phaedra wild with desire, then forsakes her. Gazing upon the young man's corpse, she cries: "O Hippolytus, is it such I see thy face, such have I made it? What savage Sinis, what Procrustes, has scattered thy members so, or what Cretan bull, fierce, two-formed monster, filling the labyrinth of Daedalus with his huge bellowings, has torn thee asunder with his horns? Ah, woe is me! whither is thy glorious beauty fled, and thine eyes, my stars?" Hippolytus' tragic end is in fact foreshadowed by the Chorus' ominous allusion to beauty's fragility and the caprice of time: "O beauty, doubtful boon to mortals, brief gift for but a little time, how swiftly on quick foot thou dost slip away! [...] Beauty is a fleeting thing. Who that is wise would trust so frail a blessing? Enjoy it while thou mayest. Time is silently undermining thee, and an hour, worse than the last, is ever creeping on."

Glossary of Terms

Alpheus

A river in Greece; also the name of a river god in Greek mythology.

Aphidnae

An ancient city near Athens.

Araxes

A river located in the Middle East, running through modern-day Iran, Turkey, Armenia, and Azerbaijan.

Bacchus

The god of wine and merriment.

Bullocks

Castrated bulls.

Cecrops

One of the mythical kings of Athens, during whose reign Athena became the patron goddess of the city.

Crete

The island, ruled by King Minos, upon which Theseus slew the Minotaur.

Daedalus

A figure of Greek mythology famous for his skill as a craftsman; he built a labyrinth to enclose the Minotaur.

Diana

Goddess of the hunt, of chastity, and of the moon.

Lerna

A region of springs in ancient Greece.

marrow

The interior of bones.

Neptune

God of the sea and Theseus' father.

Pallas

Refers to Athena, patron goddess of Athens.

Phlegethon

One of the five rivers of the underworld in Greek mythology.

Styx

The mythic river forming the boundary between the Underworld and the upper (mortal) world.

Short Summary

Phaedra opens with Hippolytus, son of Theseus and stepson of Phaedra, setting off on a hunt. He prefers the woods to the palace, and invokes Diana, goddess of the hunt, to help his luck. After his departure, Phaedra appears, racked with despair. Her wet-nurse inquires what it is that ails her; Phaedra confesses that she is in love with Hippolytus, and recalls her own mother Pasiphae's lust for a bull – a lust that gave birth to the infamous Minotaur, which Theseus himself slew. She claims she is cursed by Venus, who is angry against Apollo, Phaedra's ancestor, for having exposed Venus' love for Mars.

The nurse pleads to Phaedra to control her passion and check her emotions, but it is no use. Phaedra speaks of herself as though of a ship caught in a storm and heading for the rocks: try as she may to change course, the waves will inexorably pull her toward her doom. Realizing the hopelessness of the situation, the nurse resolves to try to help her mistress.

Hippolytus, biological son of the Amazonian Antiope (former wife of Theseus) is known to detest all women and forsake the pleasures of civilization. When he returns from the hunt, the nurse attempts to soften his heart, arguing that he should make use of his good fortune and enjoy fine food, wine, and the company of women. Hippolytus roundly rejects the idea, proclaiming that nature is where man is at his most free and innocent and that womankind is the cause of much evil.

At that moment, Phaedra appears, and swiftly collapses in a swoon. Hippolytus wakes her, then asks why she is so ill at ease. Unsure how to proceed at first, Phaedra summons the courage to tell Hippolytus the truth, hoping he may reciprocate her feelings and lend her "success" to cover up her "sins." As it turns out, however, Hippolytus flies into a rage, railing against Phaedra and declaring her worse than her "monster-bearing mother." He draws his sword on her, but when she says she hopes to die, he casts the weapon away and flees into the woods.

Phaedra's nurse hatches a plan to conceal Phaedra's guilt by accusing Hippolytus of attempting to rape his stepmother. His abandoned sword will serve as evidence. Shortly thereafter, Theseus returns, freshly escaped from the underworld. He sees Phaedra in distress, seemingly prepared to kill herself, and demands an explanation. Phaedra tells him someone he would least expect tried to rape her; she then points to Hippolytus' sword. Theseus is aghast, and immediately calls on his father Neptune to kill his son.

A Messenger arrives, bearing news of Hippolytus' death. As we learn, a monster emerged from the windswept sea and pursued Hippolytus' horses; caught up in the reins, the young man was dragged and torn limb from limb. Seeing Hippolytus' mangled corpse, Phaedra confesses the truth to Theseus, then falls on her sword and dies. Theseus curses himself for his foolhardy decision, then orders Hippolytus' remains be gathered for a proper burial. "As for her," he says, turning to Phaedra's body, "let her be buried deep in earth, and heavy may the soil lie on her unholy head!"

Summary and Analysis of Section I: Lines 1 - 423

The play begins as Hippolytus, son of King Theseus of Athens, exits the palace courts at the break of dawn with a company of hunters and hunting dogs. The offspring of Theseus and Antiope, an Amazon whom Theseus had wed and subsequently slain, Hippolytus loves hunting, and he invokes Diana for guidance and issues orders to his company to scour the "forest glades" in search of the wild boar.

After he leaves, Phaedra, wife of Theseus and daughter of King Minos of Crete, appears in front of the palace, bemoaning her fate. Her husband has been gone for years after having left with his old friend Pirithous to capture Persephone from the underworld. Phaedra has been left alone to tend the palace, and has lately felt stricken by some sort of illness: "A malady feeds and grows within my heart, and it burns there hot as the stream that wells from Aetna's caverns," she says. She finds herself unwilling to do her daily service in honor of Athena (placing offerings in the temple, praying, etc.), and finds herself instead pining for the forests and the hunt: "My joy is to follow in pursuit of the startled beasts and with soft hand to hurl stiff javelins." Wondering where "this mad love of forest glades" comes from, she reflects on her mother, Pasiphae, daughter of Apollo. As Apollo exposed the love between Venus and Mars, Venus has "[loaded] the whole race of Phoebus with shame unspeakable"; thus, Pasiphae was doomed to fall in love with a bull and mate with him, giving birth to the Minotaur. Thankfully, the wise Daedalus built a labyrinth to conceal the Minotaur; in Phaedra's case, however, Daedalus would be unable to help her: "Though he himself should return, mighty in Attic cunning, who shut our monster in the dark labyrinth, he could afford no help to my calamity."

Phaedra's aged nurse, standing by her side, interjects that Phaedra should control the passions she feels, for love can be terribly destructive. "Whoever at the outset has resisted and routed love," she tells Phaedra, "has been safe and conqueror; but whoso by dalliance has fed the sweet torment, too late refuses to bear the accepted yoke." She warns that Phaedra is on the brink of committing a terrible crime, more sinful in a way than the "monstrous passion" that gripped her mother, and that she should be wary of her actions. Just because Theseus is in the underworld does not mean Phaedra's crime will "go concealed"; her father Minos and her ancestor Apollo will see to it that the deed is exposed.

"I know, nurse, that what thou sayest is true," Phaedra concedes, "but passion forces me to take the worser path." She explains that she is gripped by a lust she cannot control, and that reason has been defeated by passion. Her nurse reflects that such love is a "deadly pest" that seems to strike the wealthy more often than the poor. Cupid, son of Venus, may be the "least of gods" but nonetheless "holds such mighty empire."

As their conversation continues, it quickly becomes clear who is the object of Phaedra's uncontrollable desire: Hippolytus. The nurse warns Phaedra to "fear and respect" her husband. Phaedra counters that Theseus is probably forever trapped in the underworld. The nurse replies that he has a way with escaping from difficult situations. "He will give indulgence to my love, perchance," Phaedra notes. "Harsh was he even to a virtuous wife," the nurse answers, referring to Antiope.

Theseus is not the only problem, however. Hippolytus himself detests the race of women – in particular Phaedra (who is perhaps the cause of his hatred of the opposite sex). He avoids women, prefers to stay single and hunt, thereby betraying his "Amazonian" roots. Nonetheless, Phaedra vows to follow him. Every argument the nurse makes, Phaedra shoots down: Hippolytus may shun all women, but that means Phaedra need "fear no rival"; Minos may learn of this, but "he will be kind." Try as the nurse may to persuade her, Phaedra cannot be reasoned with: "I yield, dear nurse," she says, before declaring that she will commit suicide. At this, the nurse switches her tack, pleading Phaedra not to end her life. She promises to help, proclaiming before entering the palace with Phaedra: "Mine is the task to approach the savage youth and bend the cruel man's relentless will."

The Chorus proceeds to wax lyrical about love's power. Cupid is "reckless alike with torches and with arrows," his shafts affecting all living beings – humans and animals alike – and driving victims to delirious ends. Even the gods are not immune – the Chorus mentions Zeus' propensity to don earthly disguises in order to possess the objects of his affection or lust, and Diana leaving her lunar perch in order to seek love with the shepherd Endymion. Then the nurse reappears and, upon request, informs the Chorus that Phaedra is in a hopeless state, awash in tears and overwhelmed by her emotions, without "care for food or health." She behaves as though dying, her "old-time sprightliness" long gone, while "her eyes, which once shone like Phoebus' torch, no longer gleam with their ancestral fire."

At that moment, Phaedra reappears, casting away her servants and their offerings of garments: "Away, ye slaves, with robes bedecked with purple and with gold; away, scarlet of the Tyrian shell, the webs which the far-off Seres gather from the trees." She wants her hair loose, her bindings gone; she wants to steal away into the woods, her left hand "busied with a quiver" and her right wielding "a Thessalian spear," as though she herself were an Amazonian. Her nurse invokes Diana, begging the goddess to soften Hippolytus' heart and make him fall in love with Phaedra.

Analysis

This section, which presents the central problem of the play – Phaedra's love for her stepson – and thereby sets tragedy into motion, begins and ends with an invocation of Diana, goddess of the hunt – and, ironically, the goddess of chastity. Wild animals loom large over the proceedings, both figuratively and literally. Hippolytus enters the stage prepared to hunt the boar, and he himself is often described in terms that might befit an untamed beast: "savage", "fierce." He is an Amazonian, son of Antiope, and thus feels a kinship to the wilderness. From the little we see of him, we can infer that he is more comfortable careening through the woods than within the walls of the palace. He is "stern" and "hates the very name of woman," in the words of Phaedra's nurse. "Wild is he," Phaedra concedes, "but wild things, we have learned, can be o'ercome by love." Thus, Hippolytus is not so much a prince of Athens as a formidable *thing* that needs to be "o'ercome" or tamed, just as does the boar he hunts.

In other words, Hippolytus' hunt is answered by that of Phaedra and her nurse. The nurse's call to Diana is not so different from Hippolytus', in that she too is seeking to conquer a living being. Phaedra speaks of escaping into the woods and pursuing Hippolytus, just as though he were prey and she the predator: "Though he keep him to the peaks of snowy hills," she says, "though he course swiftly 'mongst the ragged rocks, still through the deep forests, over the mountains, 'tis my resolve to follow him."

Phaedra herself has the remnants of a wild beast in her blood – and in a far more literal fashion that Hippolytus. Her mother Pasiphae is a well-known figure of Greek mythology; cursed by Venus, Pasiphae fell madly in love with a bull and mated with it, thereby giving birth to the infamous Minotaur. This deed is, in a way, the original sin that plagues Phaedra: "I recognize my wretched mother's fatal curse," she says. "[Her] love and mine know how to sin in forest depths." There is the sense in these lines of love as engine of fate. Phaedra falls for Hippolytus not by choice, but because she is doomed to do so. Her tragic flaw was borne with her mother – or even earlier, with Apollo's decision to expose Venus' love for Mars.

As is evident in this history, as well as in the continual allusions to Cupid as a merciless hunter of his own, preying on the hearts of all living beings, love is depicted in Phaedra not as a boon but as a burden. It is a "deadly pest," a calamity that fells reason and drives victims to rash deeds. Every nook and cranny of the storyline bears witness to this vision: Theseus is on a crazed quest to steal away Persephone from the underworld; Phaedra's blood-line is cursed by "monstrous passion"; even Diana is susceptible to love's power, as evident by her reckless affection for the shepherd Endymion.

Intriguingly, however, the nurse, old in years and in many ways the voice of wisdom in the play, argues that love's troubles hit the rich more often than the poor. "Why steals this deadly pest more rarely into humble homes, choosing rather the homes of daintiness?" she asks. "Why doth hallowed love dwell 'neath lowly roofs and the general throng have wholesome impulses? Why hath modest fortune self-control? Why, on the other hand, do rich men, propped on empire, ever grasp at more than heaven allows?" These questions are, to a degree, rhetorical. The answer lies with the form of Greek tragedy itself, which invariably focuses on the fall of the powerful. Those who are higher up can plummet more dramatically, and it is their plight that serves as subject matter to the great tragedians. "He who is too powerful seeks power beyond his power," the nurse concludes. Here, love is equated with "seeking power";

it is a conquest, a hunt, a battle. Love is bellicose – and just as destructive as war.

Summary and Analysis of Section II: Lines 424 - 834

Hippolytus returns from hunting and, seeing Phaedra's nurse, asks her why she looks so sullen and worried. The nurse replies that there is no need to worry, that the "realm is in prosperous state," and that Hippolytus should "show [him]self less harsh." He is too stern, the nurse argues, too austere; he should enjoy his happiness, rather than waste it; he should seek the company of women, share his bed, regale himself. Hippolytus responds that life at its most innocent and free is life spent in the wild. He reflects on the men and women of "the primal age," who lived "in friendly intercourse with gods." They did not thirst for power; they found all they needed in the nature that surrounded them, and they lived in peace. Civilization changed everything; with it came crime and warfare, and with those two evils, centuries of bloodshed. Hippolytus then alludes to Phaedra briefly, saying that stepmothers "are no whit more merciful than beasts"; he goes on to declare woman as "the leader of all wickedness" and points to Medea (Aegeus' wife, who killed her own children) as an example.

"Why make the crime of few the blame of all?" the nurse asks. She then argues that "Love" can often change stubborn dispositions, causing people to question even their most deeply-held beliefs. Hippolytus himself was, after all, spared by his mother Antiope, when the Amazons traditionally killed any male infants; Antiope's love for Theseus is the very reason for Hippolytus' existence. Still, her arguments fall on deaf ears; Hippolytus maintains his steadfast hatred of womankind, and the nurse comments aside that her efforts are in vain.

At that point, Phaedra appears, swoons, and collapses. When Hippolytus awakes her, she bemoans no longer being unconscious. When asked why she is so miserable, she decides (as revealed to us in an aside) that she will confess to Hippolytus, hoping that her words might sway him: she must "follow up" what she has started, for "success makes some sins honest."

After ensuring that no else is watching or listening, Phaedra tries to subtly suggest Hippolytus should take his father's place. Theseus will likely never return from the underworld, and "it is no woman's task to watch o'er royal cities." Thus, Hippolytus should assume Theseus' mantle. Hippolytus takes the bait, offering to fill his father's shoes while awaiting his return (in which he continues to have faith). Phaedra sees her opportunity and kneels at his feet, declaring her love for him. At this, Hippolytus is aghast. He cries out that he is "guilty," for he has "stirred [his] stepmother to love." Then he pins the blame back on Phaedra, railing against what he perceives as her terrible crime. "O thou, who hast outshined the whole race of women," he says, "who hast dared a greater evil than thy monster-bearing mother, thou worse than she who bore thee!"

He draws his sword to kill Phaedra, but upon realizing this is what she *wants*, he casts the weapon away and flees into the forest, crying out: "Not great Father Neptune's self, with his whole ocean, could wash away so much of guilt."

"Crime must be concealed by crime," the nurse decides. The plan is to accuse Hippolytus of incestuous lust; since Phaedra's confession was made in secret, it will be Hippolytus' word against hers. "Help, Athens, help!" she shouts. "The ravisher, Hippolytus, with vile, lustful intent, is after us; he is upon us and threatens us with death; with the sword he is terrifying our chaste queen – ah! he has rushed headlong forth and, dazed, in panic flight, has left his sword."

The Chorus interjects, praising Hippolytus' beauty but noting that beauty is subject to the wiles of time; it slips away "swiftly on quick foot" and is but "a fleeting thing." Therefore, Hippolytus should enjoy his beauty while it lasts, because even the wilderness to which he now retreats will not preserve it indefinitely. The Chorus then condemns Phaedra's wicked scheme: "What would the woman's headlong madness leave undared? She is preparing outrageous charges against this guileless youth. Behold her guilty wiles!"

It is then that Theseus appears, freshly returned from the underworld, his countenance "deathly pale" but his "head borne high."

Analysis

The centerpiece of Seneca's play, the heated encounter between Hippolytus and Phaedra, in which stepson almost kills stepmother, further delineates the division between wilderness and civilization suggested in earlier passages. Hippolytus returns from the woods and then flees back to them; civilization presents him with an unsupportable quandary. His stepmother is reduced to a position of base servitude because of her uncontrollable feelings; the "wild" impulses that rage within her are met with fear and scorn by the wilderness-loving Hippolytus. Love dissolves into violence, or at least the threat thereof, when Hippolytus draws his sword and prepares to slay Phaedra; he mentions both Pasiphae and Medea – whose sin was quite the opposite from Phaedra's, since instead of falling in love with her sons she murdered them.

When Hippolytus argues with Phaedra's nurse, before Phaedra appears on the scene, about the relative merits of city-bound or forest-bound life, nature is invoked by both parties as a model to follow. In the nurse's perspective, it is nature's way for humans to make use of their gifts and their happiness, even if doing so means retreating from "nature" as a geographical terrain (i.e. the wilderness) and returning to the comforts of civilization: "Follow, then, nature as life's guide; frequent the city; seek out the haunts of men," she advises Hippolytus. In other words, it is *natural* to be civilized.

Hippolytus counters with the opposite claim – that the natural lies not in comfort but in being *free* and *innocent*, things which the city cannot provide: "There is no life so free and innocent, none which better cherishes the ancient ways, than that which, forsaking cities, loves the woods." The use of the word "innocent" is telling, of course, as the entire play is concerned with the notion of *sinful* passion and what constitutes transgression. Is Phaedra doing the right thing by respecting her "natural" impulses and declaring her love for Hippolytus, rather than suppress those emotions? If so, Hippolytus's view of nature as benevolent connotes a more geographical interpretation of said "nature" than a metaphorical one.

What is also intriguing about Hippolytus' speech to the nurse is that in it he identifies "lust" – though, specifically, lust for power – as one of mankind's original sins and one of the flaws that precipitated a fall from grace after the pre-civilization "primal age" of peace and bliss: "Unholy passion for gain broke up this peaceful life, headlong wrath, and lust which sets men's hearts aflame." The use of the words "passion" and "lust" (albeit translated from the Latin) is significant; "unholy passion," indeed, could easily refer specifically to Pasiphae's love for a bull or Phaedra's love for her stepson. Moreover, Hippolytus' reasoning for pointing the blame at women above all is that women are prone to adultery: "'tis by her foul adulteries so many cities smoke, so many nations war, so many peoples lie crushed beneath the ruins of their kingdoms, utterly o'erthrown." Thus, lust once again serves as catalyst of destruction, and lies at the root cause of civilization's evils.

When the face-off between stepson and stepmother finally occurs, it bristles with tension. It is a moment of high drama, but also one tinged with profound confusion. Much of Greek tragedy, from which Seneca borrowed, is deeply concerned with familial ties and the responsibilities that come with them; these responsibilities often breed calamity, and thus most tragedy is *domestic*, occurring not so much between houses as *within* a single house. (Consider Medea, driven to slay her own children; or Oedipus, who unwittingly kills his father and marries his mother.) *Phaedra*, modeled after the original Greek tale and Euripides' version of it (titled *Hippolytus*), is no exception, and the title character's confession of her love to Hippolytus betrays an impossible desire to do away with family ties. (Nowhere but in Greek tragedy does the notion of "family ties" continually ring with so much foreboding.) When called "mother" by Hippolytus, Phaedra makes as if she feels unworthy of the name – but she is also just as clearly trying to escape the shackles the name represents. As mother to Hippolytus, she cannot love him; as his "slave," she can. Family ties are inextricably wound up and confused in these passages: Hippolytus, when resuscitating Phaedra from her swoon, calls her "my daughter," and Phaedra later asks him to call her "sister."

The larger point is that the love between stepmother and stepson has confounded and blurred the boundaries of their relationship, as defined by precise nomenclature. In the following passage, consider the ways in which Phaedra strives to define a new identity for herself and a new *name* for her relationship to her object of her lust: "Mother – that name is too proud and high; a humbler name better suits my feelings. Call me sister, Hippolytus, or slave – yes, slave is better; I will endure servitude." Her tragedy lies, therefore, precisely in her role – as dictated more by civilization than by biology in this case, since she did not give birth to Hippolytus – as mother.

Summary and Analysis of Section III: Lines 835 - 1280

Appearing in front of the palace, Theseus proclaims that he has escaped the underworld but has lost his "old-time vigor." His steps faltering, his voice wavering, he asks: "But what is this tearful outcry that strikes my ears?" The nurse comes to inform him of Phaedra's plight: "she scorns our tears," she says, "and is on the very edge of death."

Theseus demands why Phaedra has resolved to die, especially now that her long-gone husband has come back to her. The nurse explains that Phaedra is telling no one the cause of her grief. Theseus opens the doors to the palace and sees Phaedra clutching a sword, ready to slay herself. He asks her why she is in such a state, but she responds only with vague, epigrammatic quips, alluding to a "sin" she has committed. Theseus asks to know what that sin is. "That I still live," comes the reply.

Rash, brimming with emotion, Theseus orders the nurse to be bound in chains and tormented with the "scourge" until she confesses her mistress's secret. Phaedra intervenes, telling her husband that she has been raped and that the "destroyer of [her] honor" is the one whom Theseus would least expect. She then points to the sword Hippolytus left behind.

"Ah me!" Theseus cries. "What villainy do I behold?" After Phaedra tells him that Hippolytus was last seen "speeding away in headlong flight," Theseus, in a rage, summons his father Neptune to destroy the young man. (He notes that his father granted him three wishes, two of which he has already used; the third will be used against his own child.) "Now, now I give thanks to the heavenly powers that Antiope fell stricken by my hand," he says, before calling out to Hippolytus: "Fugitive, through all thy hiding-places untiringly will I pursue thee; regions remote, blocked, hidden away, far separate, trackless, will I traverse, and no place shall stop me – thou knowest whence I am returned."

The Chorus responds with a query directed to the heavens: "O Nature, mighty mother of the gods, and thou, fire-bearing Olympus' lord," it cries out, "why dost thou dwell afar, all too indifferent to men, not anxious to bring blessing to the good, and to the evil, bane?" The Chorus continues by arguing that the world order is skewed, that the good are punished and the wicked rewarded, that "wretched poverty dogs the pure, and the adulterer, strong in wickedness, reigns supreme."

Only moments later, a Messenger arrives to inform Theseus that Hippolytus is dead. As the Messenger tells us, a great storm broke out and out of the ocean's depths arose a monstrous beast, its sights aimed on Hippolytus. "A bull it was," the Messenger recounts, "towering high with a dark blue neck, and he reared a high mane upon his verdant crest; his shaggy ears stood up; his eyes flashed with changing colour, now such as the lord of the wild herd might have, now such as one born beneath the sea – now his eyes dart flame, now they flash wondrous with cerulean gleam." We learn that Hippolytus, steering several horses, kept his calm and tried to control the situation; his horses, however, broke from his grasp and scattered about in a frenzy, terrified by the monster. Hippolytus' limbs became entwined in the reins, and his body was torn asunder; dragged through the forest, he was impaled by tree branches and sliced by rocks. He lies now, a battered corpse, parts of his body still strewn about the fields.

Upon hearing the news, Theseus breaks into tears. Although he wished this death upon his son, bearing with his own ears and eyes the result of the prayer wracks him with despair. "Truly I deem this the crowning woe of woes, if fortune makes what we must loathe that we must long for," he says. The Chorus proclaims that the gods target most readily the mortals of wealth of power, those men and women who scale the heights, while "the low-roofed, common home ne'er feels [Jove's] mighty blasts."

Phaedra reappears, again with a drawn sword. She condemns Theseus for his harshness and turns to Hippolytus' mangled corpse, limbs missing and blood dripping. She bemoans the young man's fate: "whither is thy glorious beauty fled," she asks, "and thine eyes, my stars?" Then she directs her rage back at her husband, revealing to him the truth – that she had falsely accused of Hippolytus of her own crime. With that, she falls on her sword and dies.

Ye jaws of wan Avernus, ye Taenarean caves, ye waves of Lethe, welcome to the wretched, ye sluggish pools, hide ye in my impious self, plunge deep and bury me in unending woes," Theseus cries. He looks upon his son's body and calls for his missing parts to be assembled, so that Hippolytus may be given a proper burial. "[Let] all Athens with loud laments resound," he declares. Then, pointing to Phaedra's corpse, he utters the play's closing line: "As for her, let her be buried deep in earth, and heavy may the soil lie on her unholy head!"

Analysis

As is so often the case in Greek tragedy, rashness and unchecked emotion spell doom for the characters of *Phaedra*. Phaedra herself lets herself be overwhelmed by lust; Theseus does not stop to question his wife's accusations, but instead readily calls for the death of his own son, so great is his rage. Even Hippolytus draws a sword on his own stepmother, merely because of her love for him; he then plunges into the forest, without considering the consequences of his hasty departure, and how his flight may be used against him to cover up Phaedra's guilt. Compare these quick-acting, shoot-first-ask-questions-later characters to Shakespeare's rational philosopher-princes; there could not be a starker contrast than that between Seneca's Theseus and Shakespeare's Hamlet. It is perhaps the central revolution of the Elizabethan stage to posit characters whose tragic flaw is a propensity to *think too much*, as opposed to the earlier Greek model (upon which Seneca draws heavily) of tragedy by virtue of unchecked passion.

Ironically, however, Seneca himself was known perhaps more as an orator, thinker, and political philosopher than as a playwright. As a result, many of his plays can be seen as academic exercises, less pieces of storytelling than frameworks through which he can debate certain issues or establish certain theses in regards to human behavior. Seneca is a cool rationalist, and he views his passionate characters from a distance, while loading them with lengthy speeches and eloquent soliloquies.

Some critics charge that Seneca's take on Greek myths such as Phaedra tends to be heavy on speechifying and low on drama; I would argue, however, that in the speeches *lies* the drama. Seneca's characters wield language as a weapon. Phaedra does not physically try to smother Hippolytus with kisses or tear off his clothes; she instead expresses her longing through words, and it is her words that inflame him so. Likewise, Phaedra exacts her final revenge on Theseus not by drawing the sword on *him*, but by simply telling him the truth; her account of what actually happened is her most efficient way of crushing him. Even Theseus himself slays his son not by his own hands but by a speech – an invocation to Neptune to destroy the fled fugitive.

What constitutes much of the tension in *Phaedra* is the juxtaposition between rash deeds and the rationality of language. The tragic result is that Theseus is forced to describe his son's body as though he were checking off the various pieces of a puzzle or the bricks of a house. The full extent of Theseus' hasty and thoughtless decision is communicated via the words Seneca places in his mouth: "What is this shapeless, ugly piece, with many a wound torn on every side?" the once-great king asks, in a passage as moving as any in Western drama. "What part it is of thee, I know not; but it is a part of thee. Here, here lay it down, not in its own but in an empty place. Is this that face which once gleamed with fire as of the stars, which turned his enemy's eyes aside? Has his beauty fallen to this? O dire fate, O cruel favour of the gods! Thus comes back son to father in answer to his prayer?"

Indeed, the tragic culmination of the play is an "answer" to the questions posed at the outset: Phaedra's love and where it would lead; Theseus' potential return and what would be his reaction. Seneca strips the theatrical form down to its essence and reduces drama to its most fundamental component: rhetoric. The play is a prolonged question-answer dialogue, acted out within the prism of Greek mythology. Shorter than the average Greek play, with fewer characters and fewer twists in the narrative, Seneca's work is one of absolute simplicity, bounding its crazed characters within a tightly controlled framework. Therein lies the tension, and therein lies the tragedy, echoed in formal terms by the playwright's exacting method.

Suggested Essay Questions

1. Is Phaedra a victim or a victimizer?

   A: An essay on this question would examine both sides of the issue. On the one hand, Phaedra knowingly deceives Theseus, thereby bringing about Hippolytus' death. On the other hand, she is stricken by a desire she knows not how to control, receives not an ounce of compassion from her stepson, and acts to protect herself.
2. Discuss the use of language in the play.

   A: Seneca was a famed orator, and the play displays impressive examples of rhetoric, as when Hippolytus argues that civilization is corrupting and that mankind is free and innocent only when in the wild.
3. Compare Seneca's *Phaedra* to Euripides' *Hippolytus*.

   A: The gods play a more direct role in Euripedes' version (which is in fact his second adaptation of the myth, his first having been lost), and Phaedra is arguably depicted in as more modest and empathetic, less sexually charged than in Seneca's play.
4. How does Seneca structure his play?

   A: An essay on this topic would focus primarily on the Chorus as a structuring tool, splitting the action into roughly five discrete episodes, akin to the five acts of Renaissance tragedy.
5. Discuss the role of the nurse.

   A: Though at first a figure of wisdom, the cool reason to Phaedra's hotheaded passion, the nurse emerges as malicious and cunning, pronouncing her plan to falsely accuse Hippolytus. She remains an enigmatic figure, never named but a crucial player in the drama.
6. Pick one speech from the play and explicate it.

   A: Seneca's language is full of flourish, his speeches replete with digressions. An essay on this topic could focus on any one of a number of passages - perhaps Hippolytus' opening monologue, or Theseus' invocation of Neptune to act out his vengeance.
7. Compare Phaedra to Medea, another female "villain" of Greek mythology and tragedy.

   A: Medea kills her children, but is often depicted in empathetic terms, abandoned by her cold husband and acting in the only way she knows how. Both women are gripped by fury and passion, and in both cases unchecked emotion leads to catastrophe.
8. Discuss the role of the forest in *Phaedra*.

A: The forest remains off-stage for the entirety of the play, but it appears and reappears in the characters' dialogue, almost as though it were a character of its own. Hippolytus is drawn to it, flees to it when the going gets tough, and there meets his demise; in her passion for her stepson, Phaedra dons Amazonian garments and prepares to pursue him through the wilderness.

9. Analyze the role of the Chorus.

   A: The Chorus comments on the action, as in much Greco-Roman drama, but also argues certain points - perhaps Seneca's own views - and at times even offers a meta-reflection on the function of tragedy, namely to bear witness to the fall of great men and women.

10. Why is Diana repeatedly invoked in the play?

   A: Diana is the goddess of the hunt and of chastity, both themes central to the play.

Heroic Mythology in Greco-Roman Drama

Phaedra is a domestic drama, detailing the horrors that befall a seemingly stable household. One can read Greek (and Latin) tragedy as a counterpoint to the glories of Greek mythology. The mythology, in addition to describing the various tragic outcomes, emphasizes the exploits of its heroes: Theseus slays the Minotaur and travels into the Underworld; Hercules accomplishes his impossible tasks; Jason obtains the Golden Fleece. The plays, however, tend to focus solely on what happens when the hero *returns* from his adventures. Perhaps the stage was set with Homer's emphasis on the bloodshed and brutal reckoning that followed Odysseus' return home. In such works as *Agamemnon*, *Medea*, and *Phaedra*, a king or hero regains his abode only to find carnage (or to unwittingly create it).

Sophocles' *Oedipus Rex* is perhaps the most famous example. Oedipus is well-known in mythology as the wise king who solved the Sphinx's riddle. The play, however, does not concern itself with Oedipus' accomplishment; it concerns itself only with what comes *afterward*. Oedipus, striving to stave off ill omens that loom over his kingdom, finds that he has married his own mother, and long ago killed his father. In despair, he gouges out his eyes and exiles himself.

Oedipus' is the quintessential domestic tragedy. The story of Phaedra was originally set on-stage by Euripides, in *Hippolytus*. Seneca drew heavily on this model in creating his own version; the French tragedian Racine adapted the story again years later. Here again we see the returning hero, whose great achievements lie in the past, and who now must face turmoil within his own house. Theseus learns that his wife lusts after his stepson – or, as Phaedra originally spins it, that his stepson has raped his wife. His resulting wrath only brings about further calamity.

Long-gone is the heroic Theseus of legend; we have instead a hotheaded and murderous man with a terrible temper problem. Time and again, Greek and Roman dramas cast characters their audiences already knew and subverted their heroic personae, rendering these godlike warriors thoughtless and frighteningly rash human beings. Glimmers of the old glory remain, as in the eloquent words Seneca allows Theseus to deliver, but far more present are the flaws. Theseus may have slain the Minotaur, Jason may have overcome tremendous obstacles and Oedipus may have outwitted the Sphinx: but now, before our eyes, these men are but helpless fools, doomed to sow the seeds of their own destruction.

Author of ClassicNote and Sources

Damien Chazelle, author of ClassicNote. Completed on October 16, 2008, copyright held by GradeSaver.

Updated and revised W.C. Miller November 28, 2008. Copyright held by GradeSaver.

Lawall, Gilbert and Sarah, Kunkel, Gerda. The Phaedra of Seneca. Wauconda, IL: Bolchazy-Carducci Publishers, 1989.

Mayer, Roland. Seneca: Phaedra. London, UK: Duckworth Publishers, 2004.

Seneca, Campbell, Robin, trans.. Letters from a Stoic. London, UK: Penguin Books, 1969.

Boyle, A. J.. Roman Tragedy. New York, NY: Routledge, 2006.

"Lucius Annaeus Seneca." The European Graduate School. 2008-10-15. <http://www.egs.edu/resources/seneca.html>.

"Lucius Annaeus Seneca." Moonstruck Drama Bookstore. 2008-10-15. <http://www.imagi-nation.com/moonstruck/clsc50.html>.

Miller, Frank Justus (trans.). "Seneca, Phaedra." Theoi Greek Mythology: Exploring Mythology in Classical Literature and Art. 2008-10-08. <http://www.theoi.com/Text/SenecaPhaedra.html>.

Essay: Reconsidering the Canon through Jansenist Contradiction in Phaedra

by Anonymous
March 01, 2006

In *Questioning Racinian Tragedy*, John Campbell takes issue with analyses of Phaedra that simplistically map Jansenist belief onto the play, or make assumptions about authorial intent as, "an uneasy amalgam of theology, biography, and tragedy" (153). Campbell sees the conventional Jansenist reading of Phaedra, which usually understands the play as unequivocally exhibiting a religious preoccupation with tragic destiny and human fallibility, as producing a Racinian "corpse" (154), meaning a singular reading foreclosing the possibility of renewed interpretations. Given the limited biographical information that would clarify the extent of Racine's Jansenist influence, and ongoing debates as to the relationship between such information and artistic production, how are we to situate Racine's biography and his relationship to Port-Royal? This paper argues that Jansenism can still yield intriguing interpretations of Phaedra if scholars accept the inevitable limitations of religion or biography as explanatory tools. Instead, by using the frameworks and evidence of biography and Jansenism, the contradictions of Phaedra should be explored, rather than obscured in the interest of an authoritative reading. Therefore, where Campbell, in his chapter "The God Question," feels the question at hand is whether or not Jansenism is truly an organizing principle of Racinian tragedy, this paper puts aside questions that seek a single historical truth, and reads Phaedra with the concern of what contradictions a Jansenist reading can yield.

A clear example of how an examination of the text can yield concurrent support for and rejection of Jansenist belief in Phaedra is found in the conditions and consequences of Phaedra's sin. Phaedra's "crime" is often taken as evidence of Racine's allegiance to Jansenism, because her tortuous psychological experience reflects the Jansenist emphasis on individual suffering. Phaedra's dialogue, and the way in which her lamenting to Oenone, Theseus, and Hippolytus is preoccupied solely with her inner turmoil demonstrate, "an attitude of indifference to the world and its institutions" (Sedgwick 198). Scholars have argued that Phaedra's character bears an aloof relation to the action of the play, which other characters initiate (Short 39-40). When Phaedra tells Theseus, "My sole desire must be for solitude" (Racine 456), along with her threats of suicide to Oenone, the reader is repeatedly reminded that Phaedra's isolation could remove her from the world (and the play) altogether. This reality speaks to the Jansenist ideal of spiritual investigation and conflict being a highly personal quest, rather than mediated by institutions or communities.

While this textual evidence points to a Jansenist disconnect from society, Phaedra's suffering is simultaneously a connection to society, which undermines a Jansenist reading. Phaedra's "bitter secret" (Racine 454) is that she is on the verge of both adultery and incest. In fact, Racine labels her feelings an "unlawful passion" (446), showing that Phaedra's crime can only be understood as a product of the law. The pandemonium created in Phaedra's psyche by the prospect of transgressing social institutions reveals a momentous deference to those institutions. The law emerges as a moral authority in the play, conflicting with the Jansenist priority attributed to divine authority and willingness to prioritize, "the interests of the individual above the interests of society" (Sedgwick 196). Jansenist followers in the past have prioritized the individual's well-being even over the good of the religious community at Port-Royal (Sedgwick 197), and have been so, "preoccupied with their own lives" (Sedgwick 198), as to decline involvement with the state or Church at a time when other religious groups were in bitter conflict with these institutions. However, Phaedra's suffering in part results from her recognizing the suffering and dissolution submitting to her passion will bring to the society and family if she transgresses the taboos of incest and adultery. We see that Phaedra, particularly in this problem of what the tragic heroine's suffering means and how it is experienced, at once contains the seeds for readings for and against Jansenist interpretation.

Racinian scholarship that replicates the canonical consensus of Phaedra as a recitation of Jansenist morality must elude contradiction in order to preserve such a reading. Short's analysis of Phaedra, which is a conventional interpretation granting Phaedra the most importance of any character and rendering her struggle an almost entirely internal one, contains two moments of recognition of the ways the play actually may not entirely adhere to this canonical explanation. First, he notes that there is a conspicuous lack of, "true monologue in which a character explores a state of mind" (Short 33). Second, Short contextualizes Phaedra's passion, recognizing it is incestuous because, "the world in which the events of the play take place" (36) define it as such. Here, there is potential for Short to examine how the conventions of the play (the absence of monologue) contradict the well-received idea that Phaedra is an isolated character, and at how social conventions (the law) precipitate Phaedra's understanding of her own transgression. However, in both these instances, the analysis opts to overlook the potential for alternative readings these observations pose. Short only "wonders" (33) at Racine's choice not to use monologue and ultimately sees Phaedra's crime as entirely "within herself" (37), choosing to gloss over contradictions in order to preserve the standard exegesis. This omission of incongruity seems to be the culprit in Campbell's frustration with the way Racine has been rendered a lifeless "corpse" (154).

The denial of contradiction in favor of a cohesive vision of Phaedra as demonstrating a Jansenist world-view has been legitimated primarily by invoking biographical evidence from Racine's association with the religious sect. The Worthen introduction to Phaedra states confidently that "Racine's education at Port-Royal played a decisive role in his intellectual life and in the course of his career as a dramatist" (444), and primes new readers to interpret Phaedra through, "the philosophical themes of Jansenist belief" (444). When the textual evidence seems to contain incongruities (as Short observes), sparse biographical facts are usually used as additional evidence that allows the idea that Racine wrote a Jansenist play to win out. But, do these bits of biography really confirm a Jansenist reading? While the historical support is limited, there is a more troubling assumption that a, "pervasive influence" (Worthen 444) from a religion means only that the beliefs of that religion are then transmitted through the author's artistic expression. Using this model, scholars assume that if Racine was at one point a Jansenist, then his tragedies unmistakably convey Jansenist standards.

Convincingly, Campbell casts considerable doubt on past readings of Phaedra that label it solely a product of Jansenism, and take for granted that Racine's relationship to Port-Royal would with out question lead to plays that unproblematically espouse Jansenist action and belief. Yet, this paper parts with Campbell in finding the question of whether one should categorically be for or against a Jansenist reading to inadequately contest how Racine becomes a "dead body" (154). Though we have little biographical information detailing Racine's Jansenism, we are able to assume that Racine's relationship to that theology would not be so simplistic as to be either a whole hearted embrace-producing works that unequivocally and (in every aspect) without contradiction espose Jansenism; or a complete break, rejection-yielding texts where Jansenism has no presence at all. If Phaedra can be read both in favor of, and against the beliefs of Jansenism, perhaps it is productive to embrace both readings in order to generate new questions about the text. Understanding a singular reading as only that, and the impossibility of full biographical accounts or the excavation of authorial intent, keeps the text "open," with out the fixed meanings that would render it lifeless.

Works Cited

Campbell, John. Questioning Racinian Tragedy. Chapel Hill: University of North Carolina

Press, 2005.

"Jean Racine." The Wadsworth Anthology of Drama. 4th Ed. Worthen,

W.B., ed. Cambridge: Heinle and Heinle, 2003. 444.

Racine, Jean. Phaedra. In The Wadsworth Anthology of Drama. 4th Ed. Worthen,

W.B., ed. Cambridge: Heinle and Heinle, 2003. 444-463.

Short, J.P. "Moral Issues." Racine: Phaedre. Valencia: Grant & cutler Ltd, 1983. 32-41.

----. "Phaedre." Racine: Phaedre. Valencia: Grant & cutler Ltd, 1983. 48-73.

Sedgwick, Alexander. "The Nature of Jansenism." Jansenism in Seventeenth-Century

France. Charlottesville: UP of Virginia. 1977. 193-207.

Quiz 1

1. **Who is Hippolytus' biological mother?**
   A. Antiope
   B. the Nurse
   C. Cleopatra
   D. Medea

2. **Who is Hippolytus' stepmother?**
   A. Phaedra
   B. Cleopatra
   C. Persephone
   D. Carla

3. **At the beginning of the play Theseus is in**
   A. Persia
   B. Sparta
   C. the Underworld
   D. Paradise

4. **Hippolytus loves to**
   A. read and study in his library
   B. make love to women
   C. hunt
   D. drink and make merry with his many friends in the city

5. **Hippolytus invokes ______ to aid him at the beginning of the play.**
   A. Apollo
   B. Neptune
   C. Diana
   D. Athena

6. **Phaedra is the wife of**
   A. Theseus
   B. Hercules
   C. Odysseus
   D. Agamemnon

7. **Medea committed what heinous act?**
    A. She killed her own children.
    B. She raped her stepson.
    C. She murdered her parents and blamed it on her nurse.
    D. She committed adultery.

8. **Theseus is the son of**
    A. Apollo
    B. Neptune
    C. Zeus
    D. Hippolytus

9. **Hippolytus is killed by**
    A. old age
    B. poison
    C. a thunderbolt
    D. his horses, who tear him apart in terror

10. **Phaedra's mother was named**
    A. Pasiphae
    B. Penelope
    C. Persephone
    D. Carla

11. **She fell in love with**
    A. a nightingale
    B. a bee
    C. a bull
    D. a swan

12. **She gave birth to**
    A. Hercules
    B. Desdemona
    C. the Cyclops
    D. the Minotaur

13. **Who helped Theseus navigate his way through the Labyrinth?**
    A. Apollo
    B. Ariadne
    C. King Minos
    D. Hippolytus

14. **Phaedra is the daughter of**
    A. King Palazzar
    B. King Petruchus
    C. King Minos
    D. King Liobly

15. **Who wrote this version of Phaedra?**
    A. Terence
    B. Homer
    C. Seneca
    D. Horace

16. **What language was the play originally written in?**
    A. English
    B. Latin
    C. Arabic
    D. French

17. **Which French playwright later adapted the story?**
    A. Moliere
    B. Antonin Artaud
    C. Corneille
    D. Racine

18. **Phaedra falls in love with**
    A. Brutus
    B. Antiope
    C. Cassius
    D. Hippolytus

19. **Theseus calls upon _______ to kill Hippolytus**

   A. Neptune
   B. Jupiter
   C. Mercury
   D. Pluto

20. **Phaedra's ancestor is**

   A. Apollo
   B. Zeus
   C. Diana
   D. Athena

21. **That ancestor exposed the love between Venus and**

   A. Troilus
   B. Endymion
   C. Cleopatra
   D. Mars

22. **Diana fell in love with the shepherd**

   A. Horacles
   B. Endymion
   C. Petraeus
   D. Derek

23. **Hippolytus reacts to Phaedra's confession by**

   A. drawing a sword on her
   B. thanking her for her honesty
   C. raping her
   D. hugging her

24. **Shortly thereafter he**

   A. rapes Phaedra
   B. flees into the woods
   C. commits suicide
   D. confronts Theseus

25. **Only moments later Theseus returns from**

A. Sparta

B. Knossos

C. the Underworld

D. Crete

Quiz 1 Answer Key

1. **(A)** Antiope
2. **(A)** Phaedra
3. **(C)** the Underworld
4. **(C)** hunt
5. **(C)** Diana
6. **(A)** Theseus
7. **(A)** She killed her own children.
8. **(B)** Neptune
9. **(D)** his horses, who tear him apart in terror
10. **(A)** Pasiphae
11. **(C)** a bull
12. **(D)** the Minotaur
13. **(B)** Ariadne
14. **(C)** King Minos
15. **(C)** Seneca
16. **(B)** Latin
17. **(D)** Racine
18. **(D)** Hippolytus
19. **(A)** Neptune
20. **(A)** Apollo
21. **(D)** Mars
22. **(B)** Endymion
23. **(A)** drawing a sword on her
24. **(B)** flees into the woods
25. **(C)** the Underworld

Quiz 2

1. **The action of the play takes place in**
    A. Thebes
    B. Athens
    C. Rome
    D. Paris

2. **Seneca drew heavily from which Greek playwright's version of the same story?**
    A. Euripides
    B. Sophocles
    C. Aeschylus
    D. none of the above

3. **That Greek playwright's version was entitled**
    A. Theseus
    B. Oedipus Rex
    C. Hippolytus
    D. none of the above

4. **Hippolytus leaves behind his**
    A. shield
    B. gun
    C. robe
    D. sword

5. **Upon learning that Hippolytus has raped Phaedra, Theseus**
    A. consults the Oracle for advice
    B. kills Phaedra to save her honor
    C. calls upon his father to kill him
    D. does nothing

6. **The action of the play is confined to the span of**
    A. one day
    B. one week
    C. one year
    D. one month

7. **"Love's is, I think, the mightiest sovereignty over me, and I fear no lord's return." Name the speaker.**
    A. Phaedra
    B. Theseus
    C. Phaedra's nurse
    D. the Chorus

8. **"Why dost thou shun the sweet boon of life restored?" Name the speaker.**
    A. Phaedra
    B. Theseus
    C. the Nurse
    D. Hippolytus

9. **To whom is the speaker speaking?**
    A. Phaedra
    B. the Nurse
    C. Hippolytus
    D. Cesare Borgia

10. **What has just happened?**
    A. Hippolytus' corpse has just arrived.
    B. Phaedra has just fainted.
    C. Phaedra has just told Hippolytus she loves him.
    D. Theseus has just returned.

11. **What was Seneca's full name?**
    A. Seneca the Hairy Foot
    B. Lucius Annaeus Seneca
    C. Romulus Seneca
    D. Spenser Chaucer Seneca

12. **In what year did Seneca die?**
    A. 6 AD
    B. 65 AD
    C. 75 AD
    D. 75 BC

13. **How did he die?**

A. He was thrown off a rock.
B. He died in battle.
C. He was tried for treason and hung.
D. He killed himself, at the request of Emperor Nero.

14. **"She persists in silence. Then by scourge and bonds shall her old nurse reveal whatever she will not tell." Name the speaker.**

A. Phaedra
B. Theseus
C. Hercules
D. Hippolytus

15. **Who is "she"?**

A. Phaedra
B. Antiope
C. Pasiphae
D. Medea

16. **What is "she" about to tell the speaker?**

A. That the speaker's father is dead.
B. That she has been visited by a Messenger.
C. That war has been declared.
D. That Hippolytus raped her.

17. **"Be firm, my trembling hands, for your sad duty." Name the speaker.**

A. Apollo
B. Theseus
C. the Nurse
D. Hippolytus

18. **Over whose body is he speaking?**

A. Joseph's
B. the Nurse's
C. Pirithous'
D. Hippolytus'

19. **What is the "duty" to which he refers?**
   A. To bury his son.
   B. To kill himself.
   C. To bury his mother.
   D. To bury his brother.

20. **Antiope was an**
   A. Persian
   B. Spartan
   C. Amazonian
   D. Macedonian

21. **Theseus travels to the Underworld with his friend**
   A. Odysseus
   B. Pirithous
   C. Prometheus
   D. Hippolytus

22. **Phaedra desires**
   A. her father
   B. her stepson
   C. a bull
   D. her biological son

23. **At the end of the play**
   A. Theseus is dead, Hippolytus is alive.
   B. The palace crumbles in an earthquake.
   C. All the characters reconcile and have a feast.
   D. Hippolytus and Phaedra are dead.

24. **Who of the following does NOT appear in the play?**
   A. Phaedra
   B. Theseus
   C. Hercules
   D. Hippolytus

25. **Which of the following gods physically appears in the play?**

A. Apollo

B. no gods physically appear in the play, they are only referred to

C. Diana

D. Athena

Quiz 2 Answer Key

1. **(B)** Athens
2. **(A)** Euripides
3. **(C)** Hippolytus
4. **(D)** sword
5. **(C)** calls upon his father to kill him
6. **(A)** one day
7. **(A)** Phaedra
8. **(D)** Hippolytus
9. **(A)** Phaedra
10. **(B)** Phaedra has just fainted.
11. **(B)** Lucius Annaeus Seneca
12. **(B)** 65 AD
13. **(D)** He killed himself, at the request of Emperor Nero.
14. **(B)** Theseus
15. **(A)** Phaedra
16. **(D)** That Hippolytus raped her.
17. **(B)** Theseus
18. **(D)** Hippolytus'
19. **(A)** To bury his son.
20. **(C)** Amazonian
21. **(B)** Pirithous
22. **(B)** her stepson
23. **(D)** Hippolytus and Phaedra are dead.
24. **(C)** Hercules
25. **(A)** Apollo

Quiz 3

1. **Seneca's Phaedra is a**
    A. comedy
    B. satire
    C. tragedy
    D. essay

2. **"O wife of Theseus, illustrious child of Jove, quickly drive guilty thoughts from thy pure breast." Name the speaker.**
    A. Phaedra
    B. the Nurse
    C. Carla
    D. Hippolytus

3. **To whom is the speaker speaking?**
    A. Phaedra
    B. Theseus
    C. herself
    D. the Nurse

4. **What are the "guilty thoughts"?**
    A. Theseus' lust for his mother
    B. Phaedra's love for her stepson
    C. Prometheus' lust for a serpent
    D. Pasipha's lust for a bull

5. **"Whither, my soul, art tending? Why this mad love of forest glades?" Name the speaker.**
    A. Phaedra
    B. Theseus
    C. the Nurse
    D. Hippolytus

6. **"Go, girdle the shadowy woods and the topmost ridges of the mount, ye sons of Cecrops!" Name the speaker.**
    A. Phaedra
    B. Theseus
    C. the Nurse
    D. Hippolytus

7. **Who is the speaker addressing?**
    A. his/her company of huntsmen
    B. Neptune
    C. his/her warriors, preparing for battle
    D. Athena

8. **When in the play are these lines uttered?**
    A. at the end
    B. at the beginning
    C. in the afterword
    D. in the middle

9. **Theseus is the father of**
    A. Phaedra
    B. Pasiphae
    C. Pirithous
    D. Hippolytus

10. **Antiope is the mother of**
    A. Phaedra
    B. the Nurse
    C. Medea
    D. Hippolytus

11. **Apollo is Phaedra's**
    A. father
    B. brother
    C. ancestor
    D. sworn enemy

12. **Phaedra's nurse decides to**
    A. accuse Hippolytus of raping Phaedra
    B. tell Theseus the truth about what happened
    C. quit her job
    D. kill herself

13. **"Now die, if thou art pure, for thy husband's sake." Name the speaker.**
   A. Phaedra
   B. Theseus
   C. the Nurse
   D. Hippolytus

14. **To whom is the speaker speaking?**
   A. Theseus
   B. the Nurse
   C. him/herself
   D. Hippolytus

15. **Who is the "husband"?**
   A. Theseus
   B. Agamemnon
   C. Prometheus
   D. Hippolytus

16. **"What fury pricks thee on, wild with grief?" Name the speaker.**
   A. Phaedra
   B. Theseus
   C. the Nurse
   D. Hippolytus

17. **To whom is the speaker speaking?**
   A. Phaedra
   B. Theseus
   C. the Nurse
   D. Hippolytus

18. **What prompts the speaker to say those lines?**
   A. Phaedra has her sword drawn.
   B. The Nurse is swimming.
   C. Dogs are barking wildly.
   D. Hippolytus has just been killed.

19. **Seneca was born in**
   A. Athens
   B. Sparta
   C. Rome
   D. Spain

20. **He became the tutor to**
   A. Emperor Constantine
   B. Emperor Charles
   C. Emperor Caligula
   D. Emperor Nero

21. **He was accused of**
   A. spying for the French
   B. conspiring against Charles
   C. conspiring against Nero
   D. conspiring against Constantine

22. **He was born in around what year?**
   A. 3 BC
   B. 1216
   C. 25 AD
   D. 250 BC

23. **His father was a teacher of**
   A. biology
   B. rhetoric
   C. computer science
   D. mathematics

24. **Phaedra was**
   A. his only play
   B. the only play he wrote that drew on Greek sources
   C. one of his plays
   D. the only play he wrote that featured figures from Greek mythology

25. **Seneca died by**

A. old age

B. disease

C. suicide

D. a chariot-racing accident

Quiz 3 Answer Key

1. **(C)** tragedy
2. **(B)** the Nurse
3. **(A)** Phaedra
4. **(B)** Phaedra's love for her stepson
5. **(A)** Phaedra
6. **(D)** Hippolytus
7. **(A)** his/her company of huntsmen
8. **(B)** at the beginning
9. **(D)** Hippolytus
10. **(D)** Hippolytus
11. **(C)** ancestor
12. **(A)** accuse Hippolytus of raping Phaedra
13. **(A)** Phaedra
14. **(C)** him/herself
15. **(A)** Theseus
16. **(B)** Theseus
17. **(A)** Phaedra
18. **(A)** Phaedra has her sword drawn.
19. **(D)** Spain
20. **(D)** Emperor Nero
21. **(C)** conspiring against Nero
22. **(A)** 3 BC
23. **(B)** rhetoric
24. **(C)** one of his plays
25. **(C)** suicide

Quiz 4

1. **"O ______, is it such I see thy face? such have I made it?" Fill in the blank.**
    A. Phaedra
    B. Theseus
    C. Diana
    D. Hippolytus

2. **Who is the speaker?**
    A. Apollo
    B. Phaedra
    C. the Nurse
    D. Hippolytus

3. **What has just happened?**
    A. A lightning bolt has struck the palace.
    B. Theseus' corpse has been dragged from the Underworld.
    C. Hippolytus has been killed and his corpse has been pulled up to the palace.
    D. Phaedra has killed herself.

4. **"He fled like a raging tempest, swifter than cloud-collecting Corus, swifter than flame which speeds on its way when a star, driven by the winds, extends its long-trailing fire." Name the speaker.**
    A. Theseus
    B. the Nurse
    C. the Chorus
    D. Hippolytus

5. **Who fled?**
    A. Theseus
    B. Pasiphae
    C. Pirithous
    D. Hippolytus

6. **Where did he/she flee?**
    A. into the ocean
    B. into the cellar of the palace
    C. into the forest
    D. back into the Underworld

7. **How does Phaedra die?**
   - A. Hippolytus kills her.
   - B. She kills herself.
   - C. Theseus kills her.
   - D. The Nurse kills her.

8. **"No hope is there that such suffering can be relieved, and no end will there be to her mad fires." Name the speaker.**
   - A. Phaedra
   - B. Theseus
   - C. the Nurse
   - D. Hippolytus

9. **To whom is the speaker referring?**
   - A. Phaedra
   - B. Pasiphae
   - C. the Nurse
   - D. Medea

10. **Hippolytus _____ women**
    - A. idolizes
    - B. hates
    - C. paints pictures of
    - D. loves

11. **Phaedra is Hippolytus'**
    - A. daughter
    - B. stepmother
    - C. stepsister
    - D. grandmother

12. **The beast that jumps out of the sea, in pursuit of Hippolytus, looks like**
    - A. a jaguar
    - B. an octopus
    - C. an antelope
    - D. a bull

13. **"As for her, let her be buried deep in earth, and heavy may the soil lie on her unholy head!" Name the speaker.**

A. Phaedra
B. Theseus
C. Pasiphae
D. Hippolytus

14. **To whom is the speaker referring?**

A. Phaedra
B. Pasiphae
C. the Nurse
D. Hippolytus

15. **Why does the speaker say these lines?**

A. Because Medea has killed his children.
B. Because Hippolytus has killed his loved one.
C. Because Phaedra has deceived him, thereby leading to his son's death.
D. Because he has married his mother.

16. **When are these lines uttered?**

A. at the end of the play
B. at the beginning of the play
C. in the middle of the play
D. never

17. **Who speaks of and idealizes the "primal age"?**

A. Phaedra
B. Theseus
C. the Nurse
D. Hippolytus

18. **Theseus is King of**

A. Thebes
B. Athens
C. Sparta
D. Delphi

19. **Hippolytus is Theseus'**
   A. father
   B. cousin
   C. brother
   D. son

20. **Theseus married and then ______ Antiope.**
   A. killed
   B. offered one flower a year for one hundred years to
   C. sold his soul to
   D. wrote a novel about

21. **The patron goddess of Athens was**
   A. Luna
   B. Diana
   C. Venus
   D. Athena

22. **Endymion was a**
   A. prince
   B. shepherd
   C. librarian
   D. king

23. **"Ye jaws of wan Avernus, ye Taenarean caves, ye waves of Lethe, welcome to the wretched, ye sluggish pools, hide ye in my impious self, plunge deep and bury me in unending woes." Name the speaker.**
   A. Phaedra
   B. Theseus
   C. the Nurse
   D. Hippolytus

24. **Styx is a river bordering**
   A. the Underworld and the upper (mortal) world
   B. Athens and Sparta
   C. France and Germany
   D. Spain and Portugal

25. **How does Phaedra kill herself?**

A. She takes poison.

B. She falls upon her sword.

C. She drowns herself.

D. She jumps off a cliff.

Quiz 4 Answer Key

1. **(D)** Hippolytus
2. **(B)** Phaedra
3. **(C)** Hippolytus has been killed and his corpse has been pulled up to the palace.
4. **(C)** the Chorus
5. **(D)** Hippolytus
6. **(C)** into the forest
7. **(B)** She kills herself.
8. **(C)** the Nurse
9. **(A)** Phaedra
10. **(B)** hates
11. **(B)** stepmother
12. **(D)** a bull
13. **(B)** Theseus
14. **(A)** Phaedra
15. **(C)** Because Phaedra has deceived him, thereby leading to his son's death.
16. **(A)** at the end of the play
17. **(D)** Hippolytus
18. **(B)** Athens
19. **(D)** son
20. **(A)** killed
21. **(D)** Athena
22. **(B)** shepherd
23. **(B)** Theseus
24. **(A)** the Underworld and the upper (mortal) world
25. **(B)** She falls upon her sword.

ClassicNotes

GradeSaver™

Getting you the grade since 1999™

Printed in Great Britain
by Amazon

40585129R00046